Community

We Are Not Alone

The Lutheran Spirituality Series

Naomichi Masaki

I0805640

CONCORDIA PUBLISHING HOUSE · SAINT LOUIS

3558 S. Jefferson Ave., St. Louis, MO 63118-3968
1-800-325-3040 • www.cph.org

Written by Naomichi Masaki

Edited by Robert C. Baker

Quotations marked AE are from Luther's Works, American Edition (56 vols.; St. Louis: Concordia Publishing House and Philadelphia: Fortress Press, 1955–86).

The Ignatius quotation on page 9–10 was translated from *The Apostolic Fathers*, vol. 1, trans. by the author.

Quotations marked *Glaubenslehre* on page 17 and 45 were translated from *Der christliche Glaube nach den Grundsazen der evangelischen Kirche*, second edition, trans. by the author.

This publication may be available in braille, in large print, or on cassette tape for the visually impaired. Please allow 8 to 12 weeks for delivery. Write to Lutheran Blind Mission, 7550 Watson Rd., St. Louis, MO 63119-4409; call toll-free 1-888-215-2455; or visit the Web site: www.blindmission.org.

Manufactured in the United States of America

1 2 3 4 5 6 7 8 9 10 16 15 14 13 12 11 10 09 08 07

Contents

Hymnal Key

LSB=Lutheran Service Book
ELH=Evangelical Lutheran Hymnary
HS98=Hymnal Supplement 98
CW=Christian Worship
LW=Lutheran Worship
LBW=Lutheran Book of Worship
TLH=The Lutheran Hymnal

About This Series

In the West, spirituality is as nebulous as it is popular. Having succumbed to humanism, rationalism, and Darwinism, communities once known for a genuine Christian piety now provide a fertile breeding ground for self-made theologies, Eastern religions, the worship of science and technology, or even a resuscitation of the old pagan gods. In a highly competitive environment, each of these spiritual philosophies seeks to fill the vacuum left by the seemingly departed Christian spirit.

Even among faithful Christians, and at other times and places, spirituality has run the gamut from the mystical to the almost sterile. From the emotional to the pragmatic, the experiential to the cerebral, the all-too-human desire to experience (and control!) the divine has proven to be especially resilient. Influenced by modernism, postmodernism, and whatever comes next, even those who try faithfully to follow Jesus Christ may find defining *spirituality*, or at least what is distinctively Christian about their own beliefs and practices, a significant challenge.

Do Lutheran Christians have a spirituality? Indeed they do! This adult Bible study series explores the rich depths of a distinctively Lutheran spirituality that begins in Baptism and is founded upon God's Word. There, the incarnate, crucified, and resurrected Lord proclaims His victory over sin, death, and the devil, and from there flows the proclamation of His Gospel and the administration of His Sacraments. It is through these means presented within the liturgy of His Church that Christ communicates not merely spiritual energies, an emotional high, a method of reasoning, or a stringent morality, but truly Himself—God in human flesh.

Written by respected Lutheran scholars in the United States and Australia, this adult Bible study series emphasizes the Bible, Luther's catechism, and the Lutheran hymnal as concrete and integral resources for a truly Lutheran spirituality. May God richly bless those who study His Word, and through His Word may they experience the genuinely enlightening and life-giving spirituality found only in the life, death, and resurrection of our Lord and Savior, Jesus Christ.

The Editor

Participant Introduction

"I'm a spiritual person, but I'm not religious." Have you ever heard someone say something like this? Perhaps you have had the same thought yourself. Today, many people feel that no organized religion empowers them to be healthy, renewed, or growing human beings—or even Christians! To them, rituals and organizations found in churches are mere empty shells.

Such observations may be well-meant as one seeks a deeper relationship with God *from our point of view*. After all, we all think of ourselves as the center of the world. We like to choose what is best for ourselves. So we tend to look for a god who may satisfy our desires and wishes. If the Christian God doesn't deliver or meet our specifications, we seek another option to support and cultivate our own "spirituality." Further, in a religiously diverse environment, Christians even routinely switch denominational affiliations. They float around, attempting to find a place that they can call home.

Jesus says: "I came that they may have life and have it abundantly" (John 10:10). This little book will expound a Lutheran conviction that we do have abundant life given in the Church. Lutherans confess in Article VII of the Augsburg Confession that the Church is the assembly of all believers "in which the Gospel is purely taught and the Sacraments are correctly administered." It answers the questions: "Where is the Church?" and "Where can I find a church home?" Lutherans confess that a true Church is not measured by "my taste" or "my sincerest spirituality"; rather, the Church is where our crucified and risen Lord Jesus lives and gives His abundant gifts.

Jesus, who showed His love at Calvary, bids you come to His Church. Connected with Him, our lives will ever be "full of sap and green" (Psalm 92:14). Discover the richness and joy that is found in the Lord's Church alone and the life that is lived there together as Christians in community.

To prepare for "Where Christ Is, There Is the Church," read Acts 1 and 2.

Where Christ Is, There Is the Church

I believe that I cannot by my own reason or strength believe in Jesus Christ, my Lord, or come to Him. But the Holy Spirit has called me through the Gospel, enlightened me with His gifts, sanctified and kept me in the true faith. In the same way He calls, gathers, enlightens, and sanctifies the whole Christian Church on earth and keeps it with Jesus Christ in the one true faith. In this Christian Church He daily and richly forgives all my sins and the sins of all believers. On the Last Day He will raise up me and all the dead and will give eternal life to me and to all believers in Christ. This is most certainly true.

Martin Luther, The Small Catechism

For some people, the Church is an institution with a certain hierarchy and distinguished buildings. For others, the Church is a gathering of like-minded religious people. For still others, the Church is a fellowship that works toward a common goal. Martin Luther confessed differently. For him, the Church is believers who have been called, enlightened, and sanctified by the Holy Spirit through the Gospel, and the place where our sins are daily and richly forgiven.

1. Among the many denominations and churches in our day, which seem to attract the most people and why? Why do you attend the church that you are attending now?

Jesus Continues His Own Ministry

As a preparation for our inquiry into the New Testament Church, it may be helpful first to see the big picture.

2. Read Acts 1 and 2, then summarize the verses below:

a. Acts 1:1–2

b. Acts 1:3–5

c. Acts 1:6–11

d. Acts 1:12–26

e. Acts 2:1–13

f. Acts 2:14–36

g. Acts 2:37–41

h. Acts 2:42

i. Acts 2:43–47

Luke presents the Book of Acts as a continuation of his Gospel when he writes: "In the first book [the Gospel of Luke] . . . I have dealt with all that Jesus began to do and teach" (Acts 1:1).

3. For Luke, who is the main figure in the Book of Acts? What account is Luke interested in writing?

4. What do you think is the significance of the cloud in the account of Jesus' ascension?

5. More than half of Acts 1 is devoted to the story of Matthias (Acts 1:12–26). Why was it important to record the filling of the apostolic office vacated by Judas?

6. Concerning the Holy Spirit:

a. What do we hear about the Holy Spirit according to the following passages: Luke 1:35; 3:16 (Acts 1:5, 2:1–4, 38); 3:22; 4:18; 24:49?

b. John tells us more about the works of the Holy Spirit. What are the things that the Holy Spirit rejoices in doing (14:26; 15:26; and 16:13–14)?

The ascension of Jesus and the sending of the Holy Spirit are followed by Peter's preaching on behalf of the Twelve.

7. Read Acts 2:14–37. How would you summarize the content of Peter's sermon? Why were his hearers "cut to the heart"?

8. Read Acts 2:38–41. Where did the hearers end up? What do we learn about Baptism according to this passage?

9. According to Acts 2:42, what does the life of the newly baptized look like? How does Acts 2:43–47 inform us further about the life of the early New Testament Church?

Forgiveness Achieved and Distributed

Luther wrote, "We treat of the forgiveness of sins in two ways. First, how it is achieved and won. Second, how it is distributed and given to us" (AE 40:213). To see how this is accomplished, we look to the ascension of Christ, the descent of the Holy Spirit, and the life of the Early Church.

10. Using the following passages, discuss the relationship between the Lord's ascension and the sending of the Holy Spirit: Matthew 16:18; John 14:26; 15:26; 16:7; Luke 24:49; and Acts 1:2.

Acts 1:1 (or Luke 1:1)–2:13 describes how Jesus accomplished salvation (forgiveness achieved), while Acts 2:14–47 shows how Jesus actually bestows the salvation (forgiveness distributed) that He won on the cross.

11. How does Jesus distribute His forgiveness today? Is this similar or dissimilar to what Christians today may think about how we receive Christ's forgiveness?

Where Christ Is, There Is the Church

In Acts 2, the life of the congregation was characterized by the inexpressible joy of the newly baptized, the simplicity of faith clinging to the apostles' doctrine, the awe of their hearts before the wonders of the Spirit, the brotherly love that was ready to offer everything, the prayers, the celebrations of the Sacrament of the Altar, and the praise of God.

12. Apply this picture of congregational life in the Early Church to the blessings God is giving you and others in your congregation. What are they?

13. Ignatius of Antioch was a Christian pastor who lived immediately following the apostles. He wrote, "Wherever the bishop [pastor] appears, there let the multitude [congregation] be; just as wher-

ever Jesus Christ is, there is the catholic [universal] church." According to Ignatius, where should we look for Jesus today?

Spiritual Exercises

- Be comforted by the fact that, even when we are tempted by Satan, the world, and our sinful flesh, we may still say with Luther, "*Nevertheless*, I am baptized" (Large Catechism IV 44, 77–78). During the week, pray one stanza of "God's Own Child, I Gladly Say It" (*LSB* 594; *ELH* 246; *HS98* 844) in thanksgiving to God for this precious gift.
- Luther wrote that the Church is like "the mother that conceives and bears every Christian through God's Word [Galatians 4:26]. Through the Word He reveals and proclaims" (Large Catechism II 37, 42). When you next attend church services, ponder how the Church cares for you through Word and Sacrament.
- Discuss with other participants how Jesus as the Lord of the Church and the Giver of forgiveness and life may be reflected in other areas of congregational life, including the works of various boards and committees in your congregation. Reflect the same also in your daily Christian life and in your family life.

Point to Remember

So those who received his [Peter's] word were baptized, and there were added that day about three thousand souls. And they devoted themselves to the apostles' teaching and fellowship, to the breaking of bread and the prayers. Acts 2:41–42.

To prepare for "The Lord's Giving—Our Receiving," read Luke 22:24–27.

The Lord's Giving—Our Receiving

Our Lord speaks and we listen. His Word bestows what it says. Faith that is born from what is heard acknowledges the gifts received with eager thankfulness and praise. Music is drawn into this thankfulness and praise, enlarging and elevating the adoration of our gracious giver God. Saying back to Him what He has said to us, we repeat what is most true and sure. Most true and sure is His name, which He put upon us with the water of our Baptism. We are His.

Lutheran Worship, page 6

Think about world religions that you may know, have studied, or have heard of: Islam, Judaism, Hinduism, Buddhism, Confucianism, Shinto, and any other religious or spiritual movements that are active today. This could also include many groups that claim to be Christian.

14. From what you know about these religions or groups, what is the purpose of worship? Is it to benefit the deity (god or gods)? To benefit worshipers? Both?

The Lord's Giving—Our Receiving

When God finished creating the world, He saw everything that He had made and pronounced it "very good" (Genesis 1:31). Then, He kept a Sabbath (Genesis 2:1–3). Read Genesis 2:6–9, 15–25, and try to imagine life in the Garden of Eden before the fall.

15. In his *Lectures on Genesis*, Luther noted that "man was especially created for the knowledge and worship of God" (AE 1:80). Do you agree or disagree? Why or why not?

16. Read Genesis 3:1–14. The special relationship between God and human beings was wrecked by Adam and Eve's sin. What was the specific target of temptation by the serpent (Satan)?

Despite the fall into sin, God comforted Adam and Eve with the promise of a Messiah who would be born to crush the head of the serpent. Read Genesis 3:15, 20–24.

17. Note that, while Genesis begins with God (Genesis 1:1), the Book of Revelation ends with God *and the Lamb* (see Revelation 5:13; 21:22–23).Why is this significant?

Even before Christ came into the world, God provided opportunities for His Old Testament people to receive His forgiveness of sins. Read Exodus 29:38–46 as a representative account on the Divine Service (see also Exodus 20:24).

18. Describe the chief Divine Service (the burnt offering) and note the use of particular animals, a pleasing aroma, the Lord's speaking, and His blessings.

19. Read Hebrews 9:1–10:25 (see also Matthew 28:19–20; Luke 24:46–47; 1 Corinthians 11:23–26). Using these passages, compare and contrast the worship services of the Old Testament with those of the New.

20. Why are Christ's atoning sacrifice on Calvary and His resurrection central to New Testament worship?

From Our Receiving to Our Giving

Writing about Mary's song of praise in Luke 1:46–55, Luther noted, "For no one can praise God without first loving Him. No one can love Him unless He makes Himself known to him in the most lovable and intimate fashion. And He can make Himself known only through those works of His which He reveals in us, and which we feel and experience within ourselves" (AE 21:300).

21. Mary loved and obeyed God because God first showed His love to her. In what ways did Mary's humble faith express itself in word and deed?

22. Read Hebrews 13:15–16. What are examples of God-pleasing good works? Where do they take place and to whom are they directed (see also Romans 12:1; Matthew 25:31–46)?

The Vitality of Faith

Luther noted, "It is a living, busy, active, mighty thing, this faith. It is impossible for it not to be doing good works incessantly. It does not ask whether good works are to be done, but before the question is asked, it has already done them, and is constantly doing them" (AE 35:370).

23. How do you see the gracious power of the Gospel at work in your life? your family's life? your congregation? your world?

24. After receiving the Lord's Supper, we ask God to strengthen us through this precious gift "in faith toward You and in fervent love toward one another." List practical ways you can demonstrate God's love to your neighbor.

Spiritual Exercises

- One of the results of the restoration of the Gospel at the Reformation was the participation of the congregation in the liturgy. Congregational participation means first and foremost *hearing* the words of the Lord and *receiving* His body and blood, because only then (as a result) do the gifts of the Lord flow into our lips and our works. Discuss the ways in which we can encourage each other to be better receivers of the Lord's gifts.
- In preparation for receiving the Lord's Supper, meditate on the hymn, "Thee We Adore, O Hidden Savior (*LSB* 640; *HS98* 849; *LBW* 199).
- Using a Lutheran hymnal or service folder, distinguish between the sacrificial parts of worship (prayer, praise, thanksgiving) and the sacramental parts of worship (preaching, Baptism, the Lord's Supper).

Point to Remember

Through Him [Jesus] then let us continually offer up a sacrifice of praise to God, that is, the fruit of lips that acknowledge His name. Do not neglect to do good and to share what you have, for such sacrifices are pleasing to God. Hebrews 13:15–16.

To prepare for "Fellowship as Partaking," read 1 Corinthians 10:16–17.

Fellowship as Partaking

I believe in the Holy Spirit, the holy Christian Church, ***the communion of saints****, the forgiveness of sins, the resurrection of the body, and the life † everlasting. Amen.*

The Apostles' Creed

Since we are gathered to hear God's Word, call upon Him in prayer and praise, and receive the body and blood of our Lord Jesus Christ ***in the fellowship of this altar****, let us first consider our unworthiness and confess before God and one another that we have sinned in thought, word, and deed, and that we cannot free ourselves from our sinful condition.* ***Together as His people*** *let us take refuge in the infinite mercy of God, our heavenly Father, seeking His grace for the sake of Christ.*

Lutheran Service Book, page 203

As a community, the Lord has blessed us Christians with fellowship. Through Baptism, He incorporated us into His body, the Church. We are not alone (Ephesians 2:19–22). We recall what God said after the creation of Adam: "It is not good that the man should be alone" (Genesis 2:18). We were not created to live alone, nor are we re-created to live alone, but to live together in community.

25. What thoughts come into your mind when you hear words like *communion*, *fellowship*, *sharing*, *participation*, or *community*?

Fellowship as Gift

In the first session, we observed from Acts 2 that the fellowship God gives us in Christ is established by Baptism and culminates in the breaking of bread (the Lord's Supper).

26. Read 1 Corinthians 1:9 and 12:13, 27. How do these passages fit with the account of Acts in terms of Baptism?

27. Read 1 John 1 (especially verses 3, 6, and 7) and 2 Corinthians 13:14. According to John, what brings about fellowship (*koinonia*)? Is fellowship with the Church also fellowship with the Father, the Son, and the Holy Spirit?

28. Read 1 Corinthians 10:16–17. The word *participation* (ESV), *communion* (NKJV), or *sharing* (NASB) in this passage is from the same Greek word *koinonia* as we read in 1 Corinthians 1:9. What does it mean when Paul explains the Lord's Supper as *koinonia*?

Luther explained *koinonia* in 1 Corinthians 10:16–17 as follows: "Finally, 'participation' here means the common possession in which they all participate and share, viz. something which has been given to them all in common" (AE 37:353).

29. How might this interpretation help us to more fully appreciate the "communion [*sanctorum communio; koinonia*] of saints" as we confess in the Apostles' Creed?

In the New Testament, the word *koinonia* (fellowship) also refers to the fellowship of believers arising from the fellowship that they have with their risen Lord.

30. Read 2 Corinthians 8:13–15; Romans 12:12–13; and Hebrews 13:15–16. How is the depiction of Christian love as a "sacrifice" particularly important given the familiarity early Christians had with the temple services?

31. The nineteenth-century theologian Friedrich Schleiermacher wrote that the Church "is *a fellowship created by the voluntary actions of men*" (*Glaubenslehre* section 2, 2). Contrast Schleiermacher's understanding of the Church with that presented in the New Testament.

The Life of Fellowship

A study of *koinonia* in the New Testament proves that it is a unique, spiritual fellowship that is not derived from psychological, sociological, or common-cause convictions but is a gift given to us by Christ to make us one with Him and with each other.

32. How does the fellowship rooted in Jesus, especially His body and blood in the Lord's Supper, teach us how to live together as God's family of faith?

33. What practical implications for evangelism and missions are there in the unity of the Church and the unity brought about and expressed by the Lord's Supper?

The Blessings of Fellowship

Fellowship in the New Testament sense is much more than "the voluntary actions of men."

34. Read Philippians 3:10; Romans 6:3–4; and Galatians 6:2. While individual members serve each other in holy love, why is a Christian congregation different from a support group or a special-interest group?

35. Read Ephesians 3:6 and Galatians 3:26–28. How does the Lord supply us with a family of faith that transcends race, culture, political persuasion, nationality, and even time and space?

Spiritual Exercises

- Today, North American culture emphasizes the desires and demands of the individual, often at the expense of or to the detriment of the community as a whole. In prayer, ask the Lord to help you to discern how you, your family, and your congregation might become more aware of and active in caring for the physical and spiritual needs of your community.
- If you have not done so already, commit to memory Luther's explanation of the Third Article of the Apostles' Creed.
- This week, give thanks to God for Christian community by meditating on the hymn, "The Church's One Foundation" (*LSB* 644; *LW* 289; *TLH* 473).

Point to Remember

The cup of blessing that we bless, is it not a participation in the blood of Christ? The bread that we break, is it not a participation in the body of Christ? Because there is one bread, we who are many are one body, for we all partake of the one bread. 1 Corinthians 10:16–17.

To prepare for "The Gift and Service of the Pastor," read 2 Corinthians 5:17–21.

The Gift and Service of the Pastor

So that we may obtain this faith, the ministry of teaching the Gospel and administering the Sacraments was instituted. Through the Word and Sacraments, as through instruments, the Holy Spirit is given [John 20:22]. He works faith, when and where it pleases God [John 3:8], in those who hear the good news.

Augsburg Confession V, 1–2

Our churches teach that no one should publicly teach in the Church, or administer the Sacraments, without a rightly ordered call.

Augsburg Confession XIV

Jesus continues His own ministry on earth through the Church that preaches, baptizes, absolves, administers His body and blood, encourages, comforts, exhorts, and sustains. What, then, of pastors? Let's hear what the Lord says about this precious gift.

36. Read Ephesians 2:20; Romans 10:14; and Ephesians 4:11. Martin Chemnitz, an important Lutheran theologian after Luther and Melanchthon, taught that the Church consists of *both* teachers (pastors) *and* hearers (laypersons). How does this differ from the opinion that the Church is the "priesthood of all believers," excluding the pastor (see 1 Peter 2:9)?

The Office That Delivers the Means of Grace

The Lutheran Confessions note several passages of Scripture pertaining to the doctrine of the Office of the Holy Ministry. The chief passage is John 20:21–23, which is cited in Article 28 of the Augsburg Confession. The authority of the Keys or of the bishops (pastors) "is a power or commandment of God, to preach the Gospel, to forgive and retain sins, and to administer Sacraments. Christ sends out His apostles with this command."

37. Read John 20:19–23. What is the "peace" that Jesus is delivering (see also John 14:27; 16:33; Ephesians 2:13–14)?

38. In this passage, what is the connection between Jesus' breath, His words, and the Holy Spirit?

The Lutheran Confessions also refer to Matthew 28:16–20 as the Lord's mandate and institution of the Office of the Holy Ministry (see Power and Primacy of the Pope, 31). Together with the John 20 passage above, Matthew's account has always been heard in the Church's ordination rite for pastors.

39. What is the nature of the "authority" God the Father gave to Jesus?

40. To whom was the mandate "make disciples" given? What exactly was to be done? How, where, when, and to whom?

Still another passage the Confessions utilizes to confess the Holy Ministry is 2 Corinthians 5:17–21 (see Apology XXIV 79–81).

41. Read 2 Corinthians 5:17–21. The statement, "In Christ God was reconciling the world to Himself" (v. 19), becomes the proclamation, "Be reconciled to God" (v. 20). Why are the words of reconciliation both the word of the apostles and the word of God (see also 1 Thessalonians 2:13; Apology VII and VIII 28)?

> *". . . as Paul asserts, that in the preaching of the Gospel Christ Himself speaks through the mouth of the ministers (Rom 15:18–19; 2 Cor 13:3) and that God is "making His appeal through us" 2 Cor 5:20). So in the action of the Eucharist the minister acts as an ambassador in the place of Christ, who is Himself there present, and through the ministers pronounces these words: 'This is My body; this do,' etc., and for this reason His Word is efficacious. Therefore it is not a man, the minister, who by his consecration and blessing makes bread and wine into the body and blood of Christ, but Christ Himself, by means of His Word, is present in this action, and by means of the Word of His institution, which is spoken through the mouth of the minister, He brings it about that the bread is His body and the cup His blood, clearly in the same manner as it is He Himself who baptizes, though it be through the minister, and through His Word brings it about that Baptism is a washing of regeneration and renewal" (Martin Chemnitz,* Examination of the Council of Trent, *II, 229).*

42. What comfort can be taken from the fact that, as Martin Chemnitz suggests, Christ is the one who preaches, absolves, baptizes, and administers, not through the person but through the office of the pastor?

Misuse of the Office

As we have examined above, Jesus has mandated and instituted the Office of the Holy Ministry to deliver the forgiveness of sins that He won on the cross. Attention is not directed to the pastor, but to what he is there to do: to preach the Gospel and to administer the Sacraments.

43. How does the notion that a pastor is supposed to possess an indelible character go against the Lutheran confession of the Office of the Holy Ministry?

44. How does the notion that every Christian may exercise pastoral functions go against the Lutheran confession of the Office of the Holy Ministry?

The Office, Not Persons

When we look to our pastors, we look to the office that they hold and not to them as persons. Recognizing that they are forgiven sinners just like us, overlooking their petty faults, and forgiving them their sins, we support them as they serve us. This is both our job and our joy as Christians.

45. Read 1 Corinthians 9:14; Galatians 6:6–7; and 1 Timothy 5:17–18. Discuss what we owe our pastors in providing for their temporal and spiritual needs.

46. Read 1 Thessalonians 5:12–13 and Hebrews 13:17. Discuss what we owe our pastors in terms of respect and godly obedience in accordance with God's Word.

Spiritual Exercises

- Meditate upon the hymn "'As Surely as I Live,' God Said" (*LSB* 614; *LW* 235; *TLH* 331; *CW* 308; *ELH* 417) as you give thanks to God for the gift of your pastor(s).
- If you do not do so already, pray for your pastor(s), as well as all called and contract staff, other employees, officers, and volunteers in your congregation. Ask them personally if they have any special needs to which you could attend.
- Support the livelihood of your pastor(s) and other church workers through your sacrificial gifts and offerings of money, talents, and time.

Point to Remember

Jesus said to them again, "Peace be with you. As the Father has sent Me, even so I am sending you." And when He had said this, He breathed on them and said to them, "Receive the Holy Spirit. If you forgive the sins of anyone, they are forgiven; if you withhold forgiveness from anyone, it is withheld." John 20:21–23

To prepare for "We Are Not Alone," read 1 Peter 2:1–10.

We Are Not Alone

A priest is not identical with presbyter or minister—for one is born to be priest, one becomes a minister. . . . We neither can nor ought to give the name priest to those who are in charge of Word and sacrament among the people.

Martin Luther, AE 40:18, 35

The Church does not depend on the faith of individuals but on the preaching of the Gospel and the administration of the Sacraments. Through these means, God creates faith. However, faith is never autonomous. As Lutherans rejoice in the preaching office that delivers the means of grace, they also treasure the precious doctrine of the priesthood of believers.

47. What comes to mind when you hear the phrase *priesthood of believers*? Is it difficult for you to imagine that you, as a believer in Christ, are God's royal priest?

The Royal Priesthood as the Lord's Gift

The most frequently cited passage of Scripture treating the "priesthood of believers" is 1 Peter 2:9–10. However, since this passage draws on the account of the Hebrew exodus out of Egypt, we will look there first.

48. Read Exodus 19:5–6. Most English translations render verse 5 in terms of obedience ("if you will indeed *obey* my voice," ESV; "if you *obey* me fully," NIV; etc.). But the Hebrew text reads: "if you really *hear* my voice," or "if you *listen closely to* my voice." What difference does this make in our understanding of verse 5?

49. In 19:6, *priests* modifies *kingdom* in the same way that *holy* modifies *nation*. What priestly image would have arisen in the minds of the people when they heard the phrase *priestly kingdom*?

50. Were all required to serve as priests (see Exodus 19:22, 24)?

51. Read 1 Peter 1:3–5 and 2:1–10. How does Peter connect his baptismal imagery in chapter 1 to his discussion of the royal priesthood in chapter 2?

52. What do we read about the result of the election as the people of God in 2:5? What does "a spiritual house" denote? What is the "priesthood"? What "spiritual sacrifices" are acceptable to God?

53. Peter borrows from Isaiah 43:20 in writing "But you are a chosen race" (1 Peter 2:9). The chosen-ness of Christ (vv. 4, 6) is now explicitly given to the baptized. Why might Peter have done this?

The Royal Priesthood in Luther

Luther spoke of the royal priesthood primarily as a defense against the Roman Church and its concept of priesthood. While Luther never used the term "the priesthood of believers," in *The Babylonian Captivity of the Church* (AE 36:112–13), he pointed to 1 Peter 2 as proof that all Christians are priests. Luther also cited 1 Corinthians 4 when discussing the Office of the Holy Ministry, whose office-holders are priests according to their Baptism and ministers according to their call.

54. The verse 1 Corinthians 4:1 speaks of the apostolic ministry of Paul, Apollos (1:12), Cephas (1:12), and Sosthenes (1:1). How does Paul distinguish the ministry of those whom the Lord had called to serve His Church?

55. Why does a proper distinction between the Office of the Holy Ministry and the priesthood of believers give the laity a sense of freedom?

The Joy of Living as the Royal Priesthood

In his *Retraction*, Luther wrote: "In all my writings I never wanted more than that all Christians should be priests; yet not all should be consecrated by bishops, not all should preach, celebrate mass, and exercise the priestly office unless they have been appointed and called to do so. This was my final intention" (AE 39:233).

56. What may we make of the fact that 1 Peter 2:9 is referenced only once in the Lutheran Confessions (Power and Primacy of the Pope, 69) and then only to point out that the Church cannot be deprived of pastors, as Rome wanted?

57. Living in the twenty-first century, how does the confession of the doctrine of the priesthood of believers give us a sense of joy and privilege?

Spiritual Exercises

- Read and reflect on 1 Peter 2:1–10 again. Say a prayer or sing a praise to the Lord as these words of the Lord guide you.
- This week, meditate on the following hymns as you consider your various callings as God's royal priest:
  M. "All Christians Who Have Been Baptized" (*LSB* 596)
  T. "The Gifts Christ Freely Gives" (*LSB* 602)
  W. "'Come, Follow Me,' the Savior Spake" (*LSB* 688; *LW* 379; *TLH* 421; *CW* 453)
  T. "Not for Tongues of Heaven's Angels" (*LSB* 695; *CW* 495)
  F. "May We Thy Precepts, Lord, Fulfill" (*LSB* 698; *LW* 389; *TLH* 412; *LBW* 353; *CW* 458)
- Apply the doctrine of the priesthood of believers to the life of your congregation. Think about how this doctrine may be a great blessing in our Church.

Point to Remember

But you are a chosen race, a royal priesthood, a holy nation, a people for His own possession, that you may proclaim the excellencies of Him who called you out of darkness into His marvelous light. Once you were not a people, but now you are God's people; once you had not received mercy, but now you have received mercy. 1 Peter 2:9–10

To prepare for "Church, Family, and the World," read Matthew 25:31–40.

Church, Family, and the World

> *All fathers and mothers who regulate their household wisely and bring up their children to the service of God are engaged in pure holiness, in a holy work and a holy order. . . . Above these three institutions and orders [church, family, government] is the common order of Christian love, in which one serves not only the three orders, but also serves every needy person in general with all kinds of benevolent deeds, such as feeding the hungry, giving drink to the thirsty, forgiving enemies, praying for all men on earth, suffering all kinds of evil on earth, etc. Behold, all of these are called good and holy works. However, none of these orders is a means of salvation. There remains only one way above them all, viz. faith in Jesus Christ.*
>
> Martin Luther, AE 37:364

The Lord of the Church is Jesus. He is our Savior both in terms of His going to the cross for us and His bringing His gifts from the cross to us here and now. When we have received His gifts, He continues to give us more. His giving is abundant (John 3:34; 10:10). But His giving does not stop with our receiving. When the people of God have been enlivened by His gifts, they bear fruit in their lives.

58. What are your daily callings? Take some time now to share with other participants both the joys and struggles you have in serving your family members, friends, neighbors, or employer.

Christian Vocation

When we hear the word *vocation*, we usually think only in terms of an occupation or a job ("counselor," "civil servant," "electrician"). However, the functions we perform are only part of our vocation. *Vocation* means "calling," and this calling embraces the whole of our lives. In our vocations, we serve others into relationship with whom God has called us.

59. Read Ephesians 4:1 and 2 Thessalonians 2:13–14. How is the word *calling* used in these passages?

60. How does this calling relate to your specific calling in life to serve your neighbor in love?

Luther writes, "We conclude, therefore, that a Christian lives not in himself, but in Christ and in his neighbor. Otherwise he is not a Christian. He lives in Christ through faith, in his neighbor through love. By faith he is caught up beyond himself into God. By love he descends beneath himself into his neighbor" (AE 31:371).

61.What do you think Luther means in this passage? Give concrete examples of our lives lived in faith and love.

The service of God's royal priests takes place not only within the congregation, but also in the world where God has placed them in a variety of vocations—in our families, in the places of our daily work, and with our friends.

62. Read Matthew 25:34–45. Where does Jesus put Himself to receive the living sacrifice of our lives?

63. While individual Christians are called to specific vocations, the Church is called to a common mission of edification (teaching) and missions. From what we have learned so far, what may we say about this common vocation we have as baptized people?

Evangelism and missions may be said to be the highest expression of priestly love for the neighbor. However, of all our callings, evangelism in our daily life in the world may be the most challenging work.

64. Read Matthew 5:16; and 1 Peter 2:11–12; 3:1, 15. What is emphasized in these passages? What do we learn about evangelism in our daily lives?

Spouse and Family

We don't want to exclude the issues of marriage and family in our considerations of the priesthood of believers.

65. Read Ephesians 5:21–33; Genesis 1:26–28; 2:23–24; and Matthew 19:6. How may a Christian husband and a Christian wife live from the Lord's gifts? How would such a life look different from a marriage that depends on our love and commitment to each other?

66. Read Matthew 19:14. With this passage in mind, what is the best thing that Christian parents can do for their children?

For His Church, Jesus Prays

Jesus' preservation of His Church is no smaller miracle than His founding of it, just as His preservation of the world is no smaller miracle than His creation of it. The Church can no more be destroyed than Christ can be destroyed. For His Church, Christ prays.

67. Read John 17, especially verses 9–11, 20. What does Jesus pray? For whom does He pray?

68. What does Jesus' intercession teach us about the meaning of intercession in our lives—in our church, in our family, and in our world? Read also Ephesians 3:14–21.

Spiritual Exercises

- Meditate on the Table of Duties in the Small Catechism. Reflect on the Scripture passages that apply to the stations in your life.
- We have discussed the common vocation of the royal priesthood in the Church, which has to do with edification (teaching) and missions. Think about how you may want to contribute to these two areas of our life together as baptized people.
- The vitality in our daily calling, whether it may be found in our church or family or world, comes from the Lord's gifts. Seek the opportunities to receive comfort, strength, and vitality that come through the forgiveness of sins in faithful hearing of preaching, daily remembrance of your Baptism, humble receiving of the Lord's body and blood, and the hidden treasure of private confession and Absolution.

Point to Remember

And they devoted themselves to the apostles' teaching and fellowship, to the breaking of bread and the prayers . . . praising God and having favor with all the people. And the Lord added to their number day by day those who were being saved. Acts 2:42, 47

Leader Guide

Leaders, please note the different abilities of your class members. Some will easily find the many passages listed in this study. Others will struggle to find even the "easy" passages. To help everyone participate, team up members of the class. For example, if a question asks you to look up several passages, assign one passage to one group, the second to another, and so on. Divide up the work! Let participants present the different answers they discover.

Each topic is divided into four easy-to-use sections.

Focus introduces participants to key concepts that will be discovered in the section.

Inform guides the participants into Scripture to uncover truth concerning a doctrine.

Connect enables participants to apply that which is learned in Scripture to their lives and provide them an opportunity to formulate and articulate a defense of a key doctrine.

Vision provides participants with practical suggestions for extending the theme of the lesson out of the classroom and into the world.

Where Christ Is, There Is the Church

Objectives

By the power of the Holy Spirit working through God's Word, participants will (1) see in the Book of Acts how the New Testament Church begins as the ascended Lord Jesus continues His ministry on earth; (2) distinguish the two ways of treating forgiveness of sins—how it is achieved and won by Christ on the cross and how it is distributed to us by Him in the means of grace; and (3) confess that the Church is where Christ continues His saving work today.

Opening Worship

Almighty and eternal God, we give You thanks for the innumerable blessings that, without any merit or worthiness on our part, You have bestowed on us. We praise You especially that You have preserved for us Your saving Word and the Holy Sacraments. Grant, we pray, and preserve to Your holy Church throughout the world purity of doctrine and faithful pastors to preach Your Word with power. Help all who hear the Word rightly to understand and truly to believe it. Send laborers into Your harvest, and open the door of faith to those who do not know You; through Jesus Christ, Your Son, our Lord, who lives and reigns with You and the Holy Spirit, one God, now and forever (*LW*, p. 132, adapted from "General Prayer of the Church").

Sing "Lord Jesus Christ, the Church's Head" (*LSB* 647; *LW* 293; *TLH* 477; *CW* 536).

Focus

1. Answers may vary. The purpose of this introductory question is to give participants an opportunity to talk about their views on the Church. Depending on their background and upbringing, some participants may offer answers that surprise other participants. Avoid *ad*

hominem talk (in other words, avoid criticizing persons or even denominations or churches). Permit views of the Church to be expressed, so that the participants may look forward to hearing from Scripture what God says about the Church.

Jesus Continues His Own Ministry (Inform)

2. (a) Acts 1:1–2: Luke reminds the reader that he has written in his Gospel what Jesus *began to do and teach*, and that his first book ended at the Lord's ascension; (b) 1:3–5: The Lord's Passion, resurrection, and promise of the Holy Spirit; (c) 1:6–11: The account of the ascension of the Lord; (d) 1:12–26: The filling of the apostolic office that was vacated by Judas. Matthias was put into the office to complete the Twelve; (e) 2:1–13: The outpouring of the Holy Spirit; (f) 2:14–36: Peter preaches on behalf of the Twelve; (g) 2:37–41: Peter's sermon results in the repentance and Baptism of three thousand people; (h) 2:42: The life of the newly-baptized disciples; (i) 2:43–47: Further description of the life of the baptized.

3. In Acts 1:1, the aorist form of the Greek word for "began" implies that what follows is what Jesus did and taught. A better title for *The Acts of the Apostles* might be *The Acts of the Lord Jesus*, because Jesus is the main figure in Acts, or *The Acts of the Word of the Lord*, because Luke tells of how "the word of the Lord" grew (Acts 6:7; 12:24; 19:20).

4. In the Old Testament, clouds often indicate God's glory, holiness, and presence. There was the pillar of cloud during the exodus (Exodus 13:21–22; 14:19–25; 16:10; 19:9, 16; 24:15–18; 33:9–10; 40:34–38; Numbers 9:15–23; 10:11–35) and the cloud in and over the tabernacle (Exodus 40:36–37) and the temple (1 Kings 8:10–11; cf. John 12:41). Luke uses a similar expression of "overshadowing" by a cloud (see Exodus 40:35) at the conception of Jesus (Luke 1:35). Luke also records that a cloud overshadowed Jesus with Moses and Elijah on the mount of the transfiguration (Luke 9:34). Along with the cloud, fire also indicated the glory and speech of the Lord (Exodus 3:2; 19:18; 24:17; Leviticus 9:24).

Jesus' bodily ascension into a cloud does not mean that He is no longer present and active upon the earth (see Ephesians 1:19b–23; 4:10; see also Solid Declaration of the Formula of Concord VII 119; VIII 27–30). The exalted Lord is actively and graciously present in His means of grace, as Acts 2:14–47 shows. In his *Lectures on Genesis,* Luther wrote, "But we see this glory [John 8:56] face to face. We hear God speaking with us and promising forgiveness of sins in Baptism, in the Supper of His Son, and in the true use of the keys. These Abraham did not have, but he saw in the spirit and believed. Therefore our glory is greater" (AE 2:353).

5. The office of the apostle vacated by Judas could not be left empty. The Lord had His Twelve lined up on the Day of Pentecost (Acts 2:14; Matthew 28:16–20). But, then, the Twelve soon disappeared. This is not surprising because the apostles are the ones who were *sent* by Jesus (John 20:21; Romans 10:15; Titus 1:5). As a sent-one speaks only what he is given by the sender to speak (John 8:28; 16:13; 15:26; 20:21–23), the "apostles' doctrine" (Acts 2:42) was heard and kept as the doctrine/teaching of Jesus (Matthew 28:20; Ephesians 4:11–13). What grew, therefore, was not a special class of disciples called "apostles," but the words and doctrine of Jesus—"the word of the Lord grew" (Acts 6:7; 12:24; 19:20).

6. (a) The Holy Spirit came upon Mary at the conception of Jesus (Luke 1:35; cf. AE 36:341 "through the Word"); He descended on Jesus at His Baptism (Luke 3:22) as the voice from heaven declared that Jesus was the promised Suffering Servant who was sent by the Father to bear the sins of the whole world and answer for them on Calvary (Isaiah 42:1; 52:13–53:12; John 1:29–34); with the Holy Spirit and fire Jesus will baptize (Luke 3:16; Acts 1:5; 2:1–4, 38); the Holy Spirit is with Jesus' preaching (Luke 4:18); and Jesus promised to send His disciples the Holy Spirit from the Father (Luke 24:49). In all of these, we observe that the Holy Spirit was active in what "Jesus began to do and teach" (Acts 1:1) in Luke's Gospel. (b) John tells us that the Holy Spirit's office is to teach and bring to remembrance all that Jesus has said (John 14:26), to bear witness about Jesus (15:26), to guide us to the truth, and to glorify Jesus (16:13–14). In other words, the Holy Spirit's job is to deliver Jesus. He distributes the benefits of the saving work of Jesus through the means of grace.

7. Peter proclaimed Jesus of Nazareth—that He came from the Father, ministered among men, suffered, was crucified, rose, ascended, and poured out the promised Holy Spirit. But the clincher was that he rightly accused his hearers as those who had crucified this Jesus, who was made both Lord and Christ (Acts 2:36; cf. 1 Corinthians 1:18; 2:2). The hearers knew immediately that they were guilty, which prompted them to ask the disciples, "Brothers, what shall we do?" (Acts 2:37).

8. The preaching of Peter ended up in water. Peter called for repentance and for Baptism for the forgiveness of sins. He also further

taught and exhorted his listeners (Acts 2:40). In these verses, the passive voice dominates. Those who received the Word "were baptized"; they "were added" (Acts 2:41). In this way, what the Lord mandated and instituted was done: "repentance and forgiveness of sins should be proclaimed in [Jesus'] name" (Luke 24:47).

9. The Pentecost congregation was gathered by preaching and Baptism, as we have seen. Those who were baptized held to the doctrine of the apostles, fellowship, the breaking of the bread, and the prayers. "The doctrine of the apostles" is the doctrine of Jesus (John 14:26; 15:26; 16:13–14; Matthew 28:20). Fellowship (*koinonia*) embraces either the Lord's Supper (1 Corinthians 10:16–17), fellowship among the baptized through the love gifts (Romans 15:26; 2 Corinthians 8:9; 9:13; Hebrews 13:16), or both. The "breaking of the bread" is the celebration of the Lord's Supper (Acts 20:7–11). "Prayers" are answers to the gifts of God when they are received. Acts 2:43–47 further informs us about the life of this new congregation. The baptized were moved by the work of the apostles, they were ready to offer everything, they praised the Lord, they had favor with all the people, there was profound joy, and the Lord added to their number day by day.

Forgiveness Achieved and Distributed (Connect)

10. The Lord's ascension was the presupposition of the Pentecost. Or to put it another way, the ascension and the sending of the Holy Spirit can never be separated. It is the ascended Lord Jesus (Acts 1:6–11) who continued His own ministry on earth (Acts 1:1) by sending the Holy Spirit (Acts 2:1–13; John 20:22–23). The Holy Spirit bound Himself to the means of grace (preaching, Baptism, the Lord's Supper) to do what He is given to do (John 14:26; 15:26; 16:7, 13–14). The Lord also gave the apostles to deliver these gifts; that was the reason for His *sending* them (Acts 1:12–26; John 20:21–23; Matthew 28:16–20; Mark 16:15; Luke 24:44–49; Ephesians 4:11–12; 2 Corinthians 5:17–21).

11. Luther helps us to properly distinguish between salvation achieved and salvation distributed. We confess that the Church's foundation is Jesus our Lord. He builds His Church Himself through the work of the Holy Spirit in the means of grace. The Church is not built on the basis of the religious fellowship, the act of faith, the will of man, or the holiness of our lives. The Church is not found in our

hearts and spirituality either. The Church does not start with us, but with Christ and His forgiveness.

Where Christ Is, There Is the Church (Vision)

12. Here the leader should try to help participants apply the study of Acts 1 and 2 with concrete examples from their congregation, such as the liturgical life of the church and the life together as a congregation.

13. The aim of this question is to confess the Church most concretely. The Church is where Christ is; Christ gives Himself in His means of grace. Therefore, if we want to see Jesus, we go to where a congregation is assembled in His name and is being served by His called and ordained servant distributing Jesus' gifts: the Gospel and the Sacraments.

The Lord's Giving—Our Receiving

Objectives

By the power of the Holy Spirit working through God's Word, participants will (1) discover how the power of the Gospel flows into our lives through the Lord's initiative; (2) rejoice with the vitality of such movement of the Lord's giving and our receiving; and (3) recognize that the life of a Christian and of the Church is received from the Lord through His means of grace.

Opening Worship

Heavenly Father, we give You most humble and hearty thanks for all Your goodness and loving-kindness to us and to all humankind. We praise You for our creation, preservation, and all the blessings of this life, but above all for Your inestimable love in the redemption of the world by our Lord and Savior Jesus Christ, for the means of grace, and for the hope of glory. We implore You to give us that due sense of all Your mercies that we may show forth Your praise with both our lips and our lives; through Your infinite mercy in Christ Jesus, our Lord. Amen (*TLH*, p. 110, adapted from "General Prayers I").

Sing "Jesus, Thy Boundless Love to Me" (*LSB* 683; *LW* 280; *TLH* 349; *HS98* 857; *LBW* 336; *CW* 479; *ELH* 372).

Focus

14. The leader will want to assist participants in sharing what they know about other religions or religious groups. The purpose of this exercise is to help participants realize that, in most religions, "worship" is humanity's approach to a deity or higher power. Even where worship is seen as a two-way communication between the deity and human beings, many religions (including some bearing the name *Christian*) see people doing certain things (religious acts or ritu-

als) to get God or the deity to perform some service for them. Hopefully, participants will recognize that such "worship" is quite different from what we learn of worship in the Bible. There, God shows us that He meets us on His own initiative and serves us not with what we want, but what we truly need.

The Lord's Giving—Our Receiving (Inform)

15. Answers may vary. If we understand with Luther that the purpose of our creation was worship, that is, the Lord serving us with His Word as well as all His temporal (earthly) gifts, we may recognize such worship as a target of Satan. This "Satan attacks and tries to destroy" (AE 1:146).

16. Satan's specific target is our faith in God's Word. Luther continues: "For when the Gospel is preached in its purity, men have a sure guide for their faith and are able to avoid idolatry. But then Satan makes various efforts and trials in an effort either to draw men away from the Word or to corrupt it" (AE 1:146–47).

17. God comforted Adam and Eve with the promise of the Seed, the Messiah (Genesis 3:15). He then covered them with the skins of slain animals, whose blood had been spilt. Luther notes that these skins served "as a reminder to them to give thought to their wretched fall from supreme happiness into the utmost misfortune and trouble" and "a sign that they are mortal and that they are living in certain death" (AE 1:221). Because of humanity's fall into sin, God's atonement for our sin through "the Lamb of God, who takes away the sin of the world" (John 1:29) becomes the primary theme, common thread, and consistent focus running throughout all of Scripture.

18. Although there are many Old Testament passages that discuss the sacrificial services, in Exodus 29:38–46 we may discern the following four points: (1) Old Testament worship was not humanity doing something for God, but the Divine Service that God had instituted. While most English Bibles translate Exodus 29:38 as "This is what you shall *offer* on the altar," the Hebrew text says, "This is what you are *to do* on the altar." "To offer" leaves an impression that the central point here is man's act of giving something to God. However, *to do* sounds strikingly similar to, "*This do* in remembrance of Me," Christ's words instituting His Holy Supper. In fact, in the Old Testament written in Greek (*Septuagint*), the same Greek word is used in both verses. (2) The Old Testament services centered on the slaughtering and burning of the accepted animals, whose flesh and blood

had been separated. The blood was used for purification (cf. Leviticus 4:14–16), and the flesh was burnt. "A pleasing aroma" (Exodus 29:41) was a sign of God's acceptance of the sacrifice and the people who brought the sacrificial animal as well as of His withdrawal of wrath and judgment (cf. Genesis 8:21). (3) The purpose of such sacrificial service was for God to meet with His people at the sanctuary and speak to them through Moses. The service was God's appointed meeting. The Hebrew used here indicates that it is not just people coming together as a congregation. The Lord draws His people by His appointment.

19. Since the Hebrews reading is lengthy, divide it up among several participants. From these passages, we may make the following comparisons/contrasts between Old and New Testament worship. First, animal sacrifices were the chief part of the Old Testament Divine Service. However, these only pointed forward in time to the one perfect and final offering of Christ's body and blood on the cross. In the New Testament Divine Service, the chief parts of the Divine Service are preaching and the administration of the Lord's Supper. Second, while God mandated Old Testament ceremonial worship, which was also fulfilled in Christ, the New Testament Church centered its liturgy freely on the Service of the Word (taken from familiar synagogue worship) and the Service of the Sacrament (based on the Lord's institution of His Supper). Third, the Old Testament sacrifices, priesthood, tabernacle, and temple were all fulfilled in Christ; therefore their use ceased. In the New Testament, each believer is a priest having immediate access to God through Christ, who serves as High Priest over His Church. Finally, as in the Old Testament, so also in the New: in worship, God takes an initiative in coming to serve His people with His grace. Luther writes, "For the Lord not only instituted it [the Lord's Supper], but also prepares and gives it Himself, and is Himself cook, butler, food, and drink" (AE 37:142).

20. "Without the shedding of blood there is no forgiveness of sins" (Hebrews 9:22). All of Old Testament worship, ceremony, and Law pointed forward to the coming of Christ, who is their fulfillment. In the New Testament Church, the preaching of the Gospel and the administration of the Sacraments objectively deliver to their recipients the blessings and benefits of Christ's life, death, and resurrection. These can only be—and are—truly received through the gift of faith. Thus, New Testament worship centers upon Christ: the salvation that He achieved for us and that He delivers to us even now through His means of grace.

From Our Receiving to Our Giving (Connect)

21. Mary not only offered her praises to her gracious Lord, she offered her body and indeed her entire life to the Lord's service. She epitomizes total consecration, wrought by grace, to the Lord. Luther also writes on the *Magnificat*: "'My soul magnifies God, the Lord.' These words express the strong ardor and exuberant joy with which all her mind and life are inwardly exalted in the Spirit. Therefore she does not say, 'I exalt the Lord,' but, 'My soul doth exalt Him.' It is as if she said: 'My life and all my senses float in the love and praise of God and in lofty pleasures, so that I am no longer mistress of myself; I am exalted, more than I exalt myself, to praise the Lord.' . . . She is caught up, as it were, into Him and feels herself lifted up into His good and gracious will. . . . All words and thoughts fail us, and our whole life and soul must be set in motion, as though all that lived within us wanted to break forth into praise and singing" (AE 21:302, 307).

22. The fruit of God's grace in our lives, as in the life of Mary, includes the confession of His name, both in the Divine Service and to our neighbor, and the good works, or sacrifices, we perform for our neighbor. Mundane tasks such as changing the baby's diaper take on a whole new meaning when it is understood that such is holy work, when it is done by a believer trusting in Christ's merits. Our entire lives—including our bodies—are to be "living sacrifice[s]" (Romans 12:1) offered in faith to God in service to our neighbor in love. Such good works, which the Lord both commands and enables, will be recognized on the Last Day (Matthew 25:31–46).

The Vitality of Faith (Vision)

23. The dynamic flow of the Gospel—the forgiveness of sins, life, and salvation—occurs in preaching, Absolution, Baptism, and the Lord's Supper. "Wherever that Word is heard, where Baptism, the Sacrament of the Altar, and absolution are administered, there you must determine and conclude with certainty: 'This is surely God's house; here heaven has been opened.' . . . This is nothing else than calling it the kingdom of heaven and heaven itself, for the place where God dwells is the house of God. But where does God dwell? Does He not dwell in heaven? Therefore He joins the earth with heaven and heaven with the earth" (AE 5:244).

24. The collect is penned by Luther in his German Mass (*Deutsche Messe*) of 1526 (*LSB*, p. 183). The leader should allow par-

ticipants to discuss how God's love flows to their neighbors through them, and should encourage participants to share specific examples of how this is done in the home, in the congregation, at work, and in the community.

Fellowship as Partaking

Objectives

By the power of the Holy Spirit working through God's Word, participants will (1) learn that fellowship consists in the partaking of the body and blood of our Lord in Holy Communion; (2) recognize that fellowship also consists in the spiritual union believers have with their Lord through faith; and (3) rejoice that, in addition, fellowship also consists among believers.

Opening Worship

Grant, we implore You, almighty God, to Your Church Your Holy Spirit and the wisdom that comes down from above, that Your Word may not be bound but have free course and be preached to the joy and edification of Christ's holy people, so that in steadfast faith we may serve You and in the confession of Your name abide to the end; through Jesus Christ, Your Son, our Lord, who lives and reigns with You and the Holy Spirit, one God, now and forever. Amen (*LW*, p. 156).

Sing "Lord Jesus Christ, with Us Abide" (*LSB* 585; *LW* 344; *TLH* 292; *CW* 541; *ELH* 511).

Focus

25. Answers may vary. The purpose of this question is to invite participants to think through what we normally call "fellowship." Our chief goal is that, by the end of the session, participants will be able to distinguish between active fellowship, that is, the voluntary associations of individuals (the common use of the term), and passive fellowship, the communion with Christ and each other that we receive from Him.

Fellowship as Gift (Inform)

26. The passages in 1 Corinthians fit well with Acts 2. Paul, who addresses the church of God at Corinth as the saints who have been

sanctified and called (1 Corinthians 1:2), now declares that they have been called "into the fellowship [*koinonia*] of Jesus Christ our Lord" (1:9). By the one Spirit, they were all baptized into one body (1 Corinthians 12:13), the body of Christ (v. 27). In Christ's body, fellowship is not something that we do (active fellowship) but something that we receive (passive fellowship) as a gift. As time permits, the leader can direct participants to Luther's explanation of the Third Article of the Creed, where he notes how fellowship is received by the Spirit's grace through the Gospel and not by our own doing.

27. According to John, the proclamation of Jesus brings the hearers into fellowship (*koinonia*) with those who proclaim Him and into the fellowship (*koinonia*) with the Father and with His Son, Jesus Christ. In the apostolic benediction of 2 Corinthians 13:14, fellowship (*koinonia*) is associated with the Holy Spirit. Scholars discuss whether the genitive in "the fellowship *of* the Holy Spirit" is to be understood either as objective genitive or subjective genitive, that is, whether it is a common participation in the Holy Spirit or the fellowship worked by the Holy Spirit. It should be both. Through the means of grace, we are brought into fellowship with the triune God. We studied earlier from John's Gospel and Acts 1–2 and hear through 2 Corinthians 13:14 that the Holy Spirit brings us into such fellowship by delivering Jesus to us through the means of grace.

28. Here in 1 Corinthians 10:16–17, those to whom our Lord gives His body and blood in the Lord's Supper are by that body and blood "fellowshiped" (*koinonia*-ed, so to speak). To be together at the Lord's Table is to be in the fellowship (*koinonia*). The stress is not our being together there as brothers and sisters in Christ, but what the body and blood of the Lord are doing to those who receive them. The fellowship (*koinonia*) does not come from us, but from the body and blood of Jesus.

29. Luther is right, as the word *koinonia* ("fellowship") comes from *to koinon* ("the common thing") in Greek. What we are given to eat and to drink at the Lord's Table is not faith in the heart but the body and blood of our Lord, as Luther says: "It cannot in this passage mean the fellowship of faith in the heart, for the text speaks here of a common possession which one may receive and enjoy, such as the bread and cup. . . . So it is now evident that *koinonia*, 'participation in the body of Christ,' is nothing else than the body of Christ as a common possession, distributed among many for them to partake." (AE 37:353).

While the usual interpretation of "communion of saints" (Latin: *sanctorum communio*) in the Apostles' Creed is a communion of holy persons (the saints), some scholars argue that the phrase is better understood as a communion of *holy things* (the Lord's body and blood). (For further reference, the leader can direct participants to J. N. D. Kelly's *Early Christian Creeds, third edition* [1972], pp. 389–90.) At the very least, 1 Corinthians 10:16–17 does refer to the *koinonia* in the Lord's body and blood in His Supper and, in the opinion of this writer, should at least leave room for understanding this phrase in the Creed as the communion of saints among whom the *holy things* (the body and blood of the Lord) are given and received.

30. On the one hand, the preaching of the Gospel and Baptism place the faithful into fellowship with the Lord and His body and blood. Such a fellowship then goes on to move into love and work, among which the gifts for bodily and spiritual needs of the brethren are certainly first and foremost. On the other hand, the giver in giving and the receiver in receiving become united (2 Corinthians 8:13–15). According to Romans 12:12–13 and Hebrews 13:15–16, the praise and thanks sacrifices of the Christians are connected with prayer, love gifts, and works of charity. Intimate and personal experience with the temple sacrificial services, which continued in Jerusalem until AD 70, may have aided early Christians in interpreting love more sacrificially. Love gives all of itself, including the use of one's body (Romans 12:1).

31. Schleiermacher also wrote: "The Christian church is formed by the coming together of regenerated individuals for ordered interaction and cooperation" (*Glaubenslehre*, section 115). In stark contrast, we confess according to the Scriptures that our coming together does not constitute the Church, but that the Lord creates, nourishes, and maintains His Church through His means of grace, the Gospel and the Sacraments. The fellowship (*koinonia*) among believers is constituted not by our will or even by the common faith that we possess in our hearts, but solely by Christ.

The Life of Fellowship (Connect)

32. When fellowship is confessed as something that flows from the Christian altar, we are prompted to treat each other not just as friends but as the ones into whose mouths are put the Lord's true body and true blood. In 1 Corinthians 10:16–17, Paul describes those who receive the body and blood of the Lord as one body (and per-

haps also one blood). Perhaps the Holy Spirit directed Paul to derive from the Lord's Supper the confession of the Church as the body of Christ. At any rate, Christian fellowship goes beyond a fellowship hall; it flows from a communion table (see Romans 14:9–10; Ephesians 5:21; Matthew 5:23–24).

33. As we saw in the first session, the Church's mission is Jesus' continual ministry on earth. Mission has as its purpose the fellowship/communion (*koinonia*) of the nations with their Lord (1 John 1:3; 1 Corinthians 1:9) in His body and blood (Acts 2:42; 1 Corinthians 10:16–17). Rather than following therapeutic and social science models, the Church's evangelism and missions have at their center the proclamation of the Gospel and a vibrant sacramental life.

The Blessings of Fellowship (Vision)

34. Left to ourselves, most of us search out community with people who are just like us or who share similar joys or concerns. But God loves us too much to abandon us to our own inclinations. He provides us with a deeper fellowship. Christian fellowship is a unique fellowship, because it is rooted in the cross where our Lord bore all of our sins. We experience both the fellowship of His sufferings (Philippians 3:10) and the power of His resurrection, because we have been united with Him in His death and resurrection in Holy Baptism (Romans 6:3–4). Because of Christ's strength, shared with us in Word and Sacrament, we are enabled to attend to the needs of our neighbors (Galatians 6:2), serving them in Christian love.

35. The Christian community, because it is united to the Godman, Jesus Christ, transcends time and space. We hear in the liturgy: "Therefore with angels and archangels and with all the company of heaven we laud and magnify Your glorious name" (*LSB* 208). Similarly, Paul writes, "I therefore, a prisoner for the Lord, urge you to walk in a manner worthy of the calling to which you have been called. . . . There is one body and one Spirit—just as you were called to the one hope that belongs to your call—one Lord, one faith, one baptism, one God and Father of all, who is over all and through all and in all" (Ephesians 4:1–6).

The Gift and Service of the Pastor

Objectives

By the power of the Holy Spirit working through God's Word, participants will (1) understand the Holy Ministry as a gift of Jesus; (2) recognize that the pastor is put there by Jesus to serve the means of grace; and (3) learn how best to confess the Holy Ministry in the life and mission of the Church.

Opening Worship

Merciful God and Father, through Your only-begotten Son, Jesus Christ, You have established Your Church to be a temple and dwelling place of Your Holy Spirit. We give thanks that You continue to provide shepherds to feed and serve Your flock, to which the Holy Spirit has made them overseers. We humbly implore You ever to strengthen the labors of Your ministers that through their ministry of Word and Sacrament Your people may bear fruit in Your knowledge and service and grow up into Him who is the head, Jesus Christ, to whom, with You and the Holy Spirit, be glory now and forever. (*LW Agenda*, p. 216)

Sing "As Surely as I Live, God Said" (*LSB* 614; *LW* 235; *TLH* 331; *CW* 308; *ELH* 417).

Focus

36. As usual, the opening question is to draw the attention of the class to the topic at hand. So often, we hear about the power struggle between a pastor and a congregation. "Who is the boss?" "Who is in charge?" The words of Chemnitz, who expressed what he had learned from his teacher Luther, can serve as a good reminder that the Church consists of *both* pastors *and* laypersons. The pastor is not there for himself but to serve the congregation. People are not left alone to serve the Gospel to themselves but are given the instrumen-

tal service of the pastor. The sound understanding of the pastoral office starts with the recognition that the Lord of the Church is Jesus, and that Jesus continues to serve His people with the Gospel in His Church.

The Office That Delivers the Means of Grace (Inform)

37. To the weak, vulnerable, and fearful disciples, Jesus comes with a word not of judgment, but of peace. This peace is different than the peace the world gives (John 14:27). "Peace to you" is no mere greeting. With His words, Jesus bestows the peace that His blood on Calvary accomplished for us all (Ephesians 2:13–14).

38. Jesus' breathing reminds us of the creation account, where God breathed into man's nostril the breath of life, and man became a living being (Genesis 2:7). It also brings to mind the story of the dry bones in Ezekiel 37. In the Nicene Creed, we confess the Holy Spirit as "the giver of life." Here, Jesus is doing what only God can do: He gives life to the dead. The words were the words of the Creator in Genesis 2. Here in John 20, the words are the words of the crucified Jesus. He gives to His disciples His breath, His Spirit, and His words. These are one gift, which should not be broken into pieces. His words, alive with His breath and His Spirit, bring the forgiveness by which we dead sinners are brought back to life.

39. In Greek, the first words that Jesus speaks to the Eleven are "given to Me." The "authority" is a gift from the Father. The Greek word for "authority" (*exousia*) is the noun form of a common impersonal verb meaning "it is permitted, allowed." The significant point is that the apostleship is not an office of crude power. Jesus does not pass on "all authority" to the Eleven, either. Such authority continues to stay with Jesus as the Eleven are given only certain tasks to do. The duties do not have to do with power and governance of the world or worldly things.

40. Jesus gives the mandate to the eleven apostles (to whom) to make disciples (to do what) by baptizing and teaching (how) in the place(s) where the Lord would have them go (where), until the consummation of time (when). This mission would extend to all the Gentiles (to whom). The apostles do not float about, "going," with nothing given them from the Lord to do, nor do Baptism and teaching float around as abstract functions seeking someone to carry them out. The mandate does not end with the original twelve apostles (the

eleven here). The apostles' ministry will continue through their successors as the apostolic ministry. The key point to recognize is that Matthew, like Luke, as we have previously seen, talks about the ministry and office of Jesus through the instrumentality of the apostolic office.

41. Christ gave to the Church the ministry of reconciliation (2 Corinthians 5:18), entrusting to it "the message [word] of reconciliation" (2 Corinthians 5:19), so that the apostles speak "on behalf of [in the place of] Christ" (2 Corinthians 5:20) as the authorized sent-ones, as the "ambassadors for [in the stead of] Christ" (2 Corinthians 5:20). The reconciliation of God in Christ takes place subjectively (in those who hear the message) in the very proclamation of the messengers of God. "When they [ministers, i.e., those who represent the person of Christ on account of the call of the Church] offer the Word of Christ or the sacraments, they do so in Christ's place and stead [Latin: *Christi vice et loco*]" (Apology VII and VIII 28).

42. Christians can take great comfort in knowing that it is Christ Himself who operates on their behalf where the Gospel is proclaimed in its purity and the Sacraments are administered according to His institution. Our salvation is dependent upon and is delivered to us by Christ through the office that He Himself instituted to serve out the means of grace.

Misuse of the Office (Connect)

43. There is no scriptural ground to claim that a pastor has an indelible character. A pastor is not a better-sanctified person. He is not in a higher class within the Lord's Church. Any such talk can only invite the power talk of the world into the Church, which may prompt the questions, "Who is the boss?" and "Who is in charge?" Lutherans rejoice in the doctrine of the Holy Ministry as the Lord's arrangement for the dynamic flow of the Gospel. They should never pit the pastoral office off of or against the royal priesthood of believers.

44. As the Augsburg Confession (XIV) confesses, reflecting "the sending" of John 20; Matthew 28; 2 Corinthians 5; and Romans 10, no one steps into the preaching office; men are put into it. The call does not come immediately, but mediately through the Church. If a man puts himself into the Office of the Holy Ministry, even though the content of his message may still be sound, it causes a doubt in hearers because, as Chemnitz says, "the real heart of the ministry is

that God by His Spirit and His grace wants to be present with the ministry and through it work efficaciously" (*LTh* 2:699). Jesus instituted not only functions of the means of grace but the office of preaching, which is to be filled by a man whom He sends. If a man is given profound understanding of the sound doctrine and the ability to teach it, then the right attitude, according to Chemnitz, is not to teach without a call but to seek a legitimate call (*ibid*).

The Office, Not Persons (Vision)

45. According to Paul, pastors have the right to expect that their services for Christ's flock will be fairly remunerated (Paul often did not demand his rights, however). Of course, "how" and "how much" and other such questions are answered at the congregational (or institutional) level. Nevertheless, church members should see to it that their pastors (and all called workers and staff) are adequately cared for. In addition to living expenses, insurance, and retirement schemes, this includes prayer, moral support, and encouragement for those who preach, teach, and serve us in the name of Christ.

46. Pastors who abuse their authority, who persistently teach false doctrine, or whose lifestyle betrays their confession of Christ should not be tolerated as spiritual leaders within the Church. However, those pastors who serve faithfully and selflessly should be duly honored as God's servants, loved, and, when it comes to preaching God's Word faithfully, obeyed, so that their work might be a joy (Hebrews 13:17).

We Are Not Alone

Objectives

By the power of the Holy Spirit working through God's Word, participants will (1) understand what the royal priesthood of believers means; (2) contrast the scriptural understanding of the royal priesthood with its popular belief; and (3) rejoice with the gift of royal priesthood in the life of the Church.

Opening Worship

Almighty and most merciful Father, in the waters of Holy Baptism You united us Your children in the sufferings, death, and resurrection of Your Son, Jesus Christ. Renew in us the gift of Your Holy Spirit, so that we may live in daily contrition and repentance with a faith that clings to our Savior. Deliver us from the power of Satan and preserve us from false and dangerous doctrines, so that we may remain faithful in hearing Christ's Word. Enable us to find joy and comfort only in Him and to bear our crosses with patience until the day of the resurrection of our bodies to life immortal; through Jesus Christ, Your Son, our Lord, who lives and reigns with You and the Holy Spirit, one God, now and forever (*LSB*, p. 274).

Sing "Church of God, Elect and Glorious" (*LSB* 646; *HS98* 864).

Focus

47. Answers may vary. Allow participants to share what they know about this term or doctrine. Some may have never heard of it. As usual, the purpose of this question is to "break the ice" before we look at Scripture and Luther's writings on this subject.

The Royal Priesthood as the Lord's Gift (Inform)

48. By designating Israel as His possession, God proclaimed His gracious election of Israel and its treasured status before Him. God is

not talking about the duties of Israel in the world but about their special relationship with Him.

49. The priesthood as an office had not yet been instituted by God (see Exodus 28). The priestly imagery would have come from the priestly service of the head of patriarchs (see Genesis 4:3; 8:20; 12:8) or those who functioned as "priests" already, characterized by consecration to the Lord (Exodus 19:22), the privilege to draw near to God (Exodus 19:22, 24), and possibly the responsibility of sacrifice. Since the Aaronic priesthood had not yet been instituted, and since all were not required to serve as "official" priests even then, here in Exodus 19:6, "of priests" is a figure of speech, a metaphor. It denotes a dignity and privilege that come from a special relationship with God. Thus, God established a relationship with His chosen and delivered people, who were to Him like unto priests, that is, wholly consecrated to Him. They are His "treasured possession" through hearing His Word.

50. Even before the Aaronic priesthood was established, some served in a special, "official" priestly capacity. Perhaps this is in anticipation of the service Aaron and his sons would provide later. In any case, the distinction to be made here is between the "priestly kingdom" and the "office" of priest, which would develop later.

51. In chapter 2, Peter carries the rebirth imagery of chapter 1 forward, creating "milk" imagery based on the "rebirth" of Baptism that he discusses in chapter 1. Like newborns, they should long for the pure milk of God's Word, which gives growth. By remaining in the Word (i.e., milk, 1:22–25), which in Baptism translated them into the Kingdom, they will "grow up" into salvation. Baptism permeates this section.

52. The result of the election is "being built up." The work is God's. He does it through Baptism. "Spiritual" does not mean nonmaterial, but that which is caused by the Holy Spirit, something that comes to us as a gift, that which belongs to the sphere of the Holy Spirit. Thus, a "spiritual house" is a house in which the Spirit dwells, where He does His work and bestows His gifts. We are reminded of the Spirit descending on Jesus at His Baptism. In our Baptisms, we become temples of the Holy Spirit. He placed His name on us as His chosen children. Only here we are told of the "priesthood." In Greek, it includes action, actor, and community. A better translation would be "a body of functioning priests." Peter is speaking of the priesthood as a community, a people of God. They are given to do something, "to offer spiritual sacrifices acceptable to God through Jesus Christ."

Spiritual sacrifices are works done in and by the Holy Spirit. Because the Holy Spirit dwells in the body of priests through Baptism, such sacrifices flow from them.

53. The One who does the electing is exclusively God (Jesus). Jesus is "the Chosen One" Himself (Luke 9:35; 23:35). The election of God's people is founded on and derived from the election of Jesus as the Messiah.

The Royal Priesthood in Luther (Connect)

54. In his Epistles, Paul speaks to equality of all believers before Christ and with each other (see Galatians 3:26–29). However, among those who are equal "sons of God through faith in Christ Jesus" are those whom God, through His call, has officially set apart to serve His Church with His means of grace. These ministers are servants of the body of Christ.

55. All believers are equally "priests" in the sense of 1 Peter 2. Within the body of Christ, the Church, everyone serves each other through the particular office in his or her station of life. However, the unity and equality of the individual members of Christ's body does not mean uniformity of action. Each is called to serve within his and her distinctive vocation using his or her own God-given gifts. One does not invade, so to speak, another's office and its duties and responsibilities. Congregational leaders do not belong in the pulpit; the pastor should not "run the show." All in all, the doctrine of the priesthood of believers confesses Jesus as the Lord and head of the Church, for cut off from the High Priest, Christ, priests would lose their priesthood.

The Joy of Living as the Royal Priesthood (Vision)

56. The doctrine of the priesthood of believers was never intended to support the practice that all Christians should preach and administer the Sacraments. Rather, it was to defend the Church from any kind of displacement of Christ as the Giver of all His gifts. This teaching serves to defend the Church against unfaithful and legalistic pastors. It teaches pastors to be faithful to their calls as it teaches believers to be faithful in their vocations. Therefore, in citing 1 Peter 2:9, Philip Melanchthon, in the Treatise on the Power and Primacy of the Pope, does not suggest that every baptized person should publicly preach, teach, and administer the Sacraments. His concern was

that the baptized should never be deprived of the service of a faithful pastor of the Gospel.

57. It is always good to return to the source. In the 1 Peter 2 passage, we heard such phrases as *newborn infants, living stones, a chosen race, a royal priesthood, a holy nation,* and *God's own people.* The gifts of the Lord continue to flow into the royal priesthood to enliven, energize, and shape our lives. What a privilege! What a joy! It is no wonder that Lutherans have always rejoiced in the teaching of the priesthood of believers. The royal priesthood originates in Baptism. The Church is made up of people elected from every nation, a chosen crowd gathered by the Holy Spirit, assembled under Christ the head. The Church is not just an assembly of like-minded individuals coming together. The Church is the body of Christ, in which all the individual members are incorporated and where all members form one body. The baptized are the priests who praise the wonderful deeds of Christ for our salvation and serve each other with His love. We are not alone. We are connected with Christ; we are also connected with all His people, those who are alive here on earth as well as those who are alive with Christ in heaven.

Church, Family, and the World

Objectives

By the power of the Holy Spirit working through God's Word, participants will (1) remember the dynamic flow of the Gospel in His giving—our receiving—and our giving; (2) understand the doctrine of vocation as the place where the gifts from the Lord live; and (3) serve their neighbor with Christian love in their church, their family, and the world.

Opening Worship

Lord God, bless Your Word wherever it is proclaimed. Make it a word of power and peace to convert those not yet Your own and to confirm those who have come to saving faith. May Your Word pass from the ear to the heart, from the heart to the lip, and from the lip to the life that, as You have promised, Your Word may achieve the purpose for which You send it; through Jesus Christ, my Lord. Amen (*LSB*).

Sing "How Clear Is Our Vocation, Lord" (*LSB* 853; *HS98* 879).

Focus

58. Answers may vary. The goal of this question is to help participants become aware of the fact that each of us is stationed in a variety of places for service.

Christian Vocation (Inform)

59. In these passages, *calling* refers to the salvation we have received by God's grace through the Gospel of Jesus Christ.

60. The salvation we have received in Christ, our calling to eternal life, moves us out into our callings, our vocations.

61. Answers may vary. Luther's remarks detract from self-made "spiritualities" that would be self-seeking or self-serving. Faith is directed toward Christ, who strengthens us by His grace. Love is directed toward our neighbor. Faithful attendance at the Divine Service

while caring for an ill loved-one and Bible reading and prayer at home while maintaining faithful work habits on the job are only a couple examples that may be given.

62. The Lord does not need our service. Our Lord directs us to the people who need our service of Christian love. Luther's vibrant understanding of vocation as the context for the life of the royal priesthood is seen vividly in his Small Catechism. Particularly in the Table of Duties, Luther describes the priestly sacrifices of believers without even once mentioning the word *priest*. Yet they are priestly sacrifices as toward the Lord, priestly because of the sacrifices believers make as they serve their neighbor in his or her need, there where the Lord puts Himself to receive our service.

63. We, as the royal priesthood, engage in the works of edification (teaching) and missions, because we cannot do otherwise. The direction of both edification and missions is toward the conversion of the sinner, his or her incorporation into the body of Christ in Baptism, and his or her reception of the body and the blood of our Lord in Holy Communion. "He first leads us into His holy congregation and places us in the bosom of the Church. Through the Church He preaches to us and brings us to Christ. . . . The Spirit has His own congregation in the world, which is the mother that conceives and bears every Christian through God's Word [Galatians 4:26]. Through the Word He reveals and preaches. . . . We further believe that in this Christian Church we have forgiveness of sin, which is wrought through the holy Sacraments and Absolution [Matthew 26:28; Mark 1:4; John 20:23] and through all kinds of comforting promises from the entire Gospel. . . . Everything, therefore, in the Christian Church is ordered toward this goal: we shall daily receive in the Church nothing but the forgiveness of sin through the Word and signs. . . . There is nothing but ‹continuous, uninterrupted› forgiveness of sin. This is because God forgives us and because we forgive, bear with, and help one another" (Large Catechism II 37, 42, 54, 55; angled brackets in original). Rather than following therapeutic and social science models, the Church's edification and missions are centered around proclamation of the Gospel and a vibrant sacramental life.

64. God's royal priests go about their daily affairs and business, doing their work as wives or mothers, husbands or fathers, sons or daughters, employers or employees, and so on. In various stations inside and outside the home, they are urged to lead "beautiful" lives, doing "beautiful" works, as these passages from Matthew and 1 Peter tell us (where we read "good" works, "good" deeds, and "good" con-

duct, the Greek literally reads "beautiful" or "noble" works, deeds, and conduct). By these good works, believers attract unbelievers to the faith that they hold and confess and of which they speak as opportunities arise. As only good trees bear good fruit (Matthew 5:13–16), and a branch bears fruit only when it is connected to the tree (John 15:5), the key here is to continue to be at the receiving end of the Lord's gifts. In other words, we are encouraged to be the people of God, the royal priesthood, and let the vitality of the Lord flow in our daily living in service to our neighbors both for their temporal needs and their eternal salvation.

Spouse and Family (Connect)

65. Marriage is holy ground and sacred space. In the New Testament, *to marry* (Greek: *gameo*) means "to fit together" or "to pair." "What therefore God has joined together [which literally means yoked together or paired together] let not man separate" (Matthew 19:6). Marriage is where the Lord Himself fits and fastens two persons to each other. Life *together* is a gift, just as life itself is a gift (Genesis 2:23, 2:7). Adam ruined the glorious life before God and in the world. But the Second Adam redeemed us (1 Corinthians 15:22, 45; Romans 5:12–19). Marriage is the Lord's work. A Christian husband and a Christian wife have first been fitted to Christ, and then they fit with each other. Therefore, as Christian marriage, begun by God, begins with the forgiveness of sins by Christ, so it continues, grows, and flourishes within His forgiveness of sins. It lives in the water of Baptism, feeds upon the body and the blood of the Lord's Supper, speaks Absolution as husband and wife forgive each other in the name of Christ, hears and reads the Word of the Lord in the home, and prays together as co-equal children of the same heavenly Father. Such a marriage, in which both a husband and a wife look to the Lord and His gifts, is very different from the one in which they look at each other to try to hold their marriage together with their love.

66. The best thing that Christian parents can do to their children, with Matthew 19:14 in mind, is to continue to bring them to Jesus through Bible stories and prayers at table and before bed, to teach them the Scriptures, the Small Catechism, and Christian hymns, to bring them regularly to the Divine Service and to other services and instructional settings such as Sunday School, and to model before them a life of continual repentance and the forgiveness of sins. As we discussed about evangelism, the best way that parents can serve their

children is by simply being people of God, by continuing to receive His gifts in the context of a life lived out not merely with our lips but also with our lives. Children will see, remember, and with God's grace, put into practice our daily course of living and our faithfulness to the Lord and His means of grace.

For His Church, Jesus Prays (Vision)

67. Here Jesus moves from His farewell discourse to the Eleven to His farewell prayer. He speaks to the Father. This is not a mere man who is praying. Here prays the eternal Son. All other prayers are prayers of plain people to God, prayers of creatures to their Creator. But this prayer is prayed by the Son to the Father. Jesus, the only Priest in the New Testament in the proper sense of the word, prays for His Church as the High Priest. He who is on the way to the cross, prays for His apostles: "Holy Father, keep them in Your name, which You have given Me, that they may be one, even as We are one. . . . Sanctify them in the truth; Your word is truth" (John 17:11, 17). Jesus does not only think of His apostles. Rather He looks further than the farthest times of the Church's history, over all generations, over all the centuries to the end of the world. He prays: "I do not ask for these only, but also for those who will believe in Me through their word" (John 17:20). Jesus prays for the preservation of the Church. And His prayer is heard. This is why we confess in the words of the Augsburg Confession that "one holy church is to remain forever" (AC VII 1). What a joy and comfort for us to know that Jesus, the Lord and the Head of the Church, prays for His members, His Church!

68. There is nothing that more deeply binds parents and children together then the intercession we make for them. There would be far less anxiety about our children if we would lay all our cares for them on the fatherly heart of God. There is nothing that so binds husband and wife together, that so helps them bear each other's burdens, as the intercessions they make for each other. There also is nothing in the Church that so binds its members together as interceding for one another. Paul wrote: "For this reason I bow my knees before the Father, from whom every family in heaven and on earth is named" (Ephesians 3:14–15). We are reminded of a scene from Bo Giertz's novel, *The Hammer of God* (Augsburg, 2005), where a dying old father responds to his daughter when she urged him to think about Jesus: "I am not able to, Lena. I can't think any longer. But I know that Jesus

is thinking of me" (p. 165). What holds sure and certain is not what we do to God or to each other. The most certain ground of our confidence is that we are His. The Lord gave us an eternal home and an everlasting destiny through Baptism. He gives us abundant life in His Church by continuing to serve us with the forgiveness of sins won by Christ on the cross and delivered in preaching and the Lord's Supper. Jesus is continually thinking of us. He continually prays for His Church. He prays for you! His Church will live forever!

Appendix of Lutheran Teaching

Below, you will find examples of how the first Lutherans addressed the issues of community. They will help you understand this important aspect of Lutheran spirituality.

The Lutheran Confession on the Church

The Lutheran Confessions confess the Church in various documents. Readers are asked to study the first fourteen articles of the Augsburg Confession together, of which only a few are printed here, as well as Luther's complete explanation of the Third Article of the Creed in his Large Catechism.

The Augsburg Confession

Article VII—The Church

Our churches teach that the one holy Church is to remain forever. The Church is the congregation of saints [Psalm 149:1] in which the Gospel is purely taught and the Sacraments are correctly administered. For the true unity of the Church it is enough to agree about the doctrine of the Gospel and the administration of the Sacraments. It is not necessary that human traditions, that is, rites or ceremonies instituted by men, should be the same everywhere. As Paul says, "One Lord, one faith, one baptism, one God and Father of all" (Ephesians 4:5–6).

Article VIII—What the Church Is

Strictly speaking, the Church is the congregation of saints and true believers. However, because many hypocrites and evil persons are mingled within them in this life [Matthew 13:24–30], it is lawful to use Sacraments administered by evil men, according to the saying of Christ, "The scribes and the Pharisees sit on Moses' seat" (Matthew 23:2). Both the Sacraments and Word are effective because of Christ's institution and command, even if they are administered by evil men.

Our churches condemn the Donatists, and others like them, who deny that it is lawful to use the ministry of evil men in the Church, and who think that the ministry of evil men is not useful and is ineffective.

Article XIV—Order in the Church

Our churches teach that no one should publicly teach in the Church, or administer the Sacraments, without a rightly ordered call.

Smalcald Articles

Article III XII—The Church

We do not agree with them [the Roman Church] that they are the Church. They are not the Church. Nor will we listen to those things that, under the name of Church, they command or forbid. Thank God, <today> a seven-year-old child knows what the Church is, namely, the holy believers and lambs who hear the voice of their Shepherd [John 10:11–16]. For the children pray, "I believe in one holy Christian Church." This holiness does not come from albs, tonsures, long gowns, and other ceremonies they made up without Holy Scripture, but from God's Word and true faith.

The Small Catechism

II: The Creed—The Third Article

Sanctification. I believe in the Holy Spirit, the holy Christian Church, the communion of saints, the forgiveness of sins, the resurrection of the body, and the life everlasting. Amen.

What does this mean? Answer: I believe that I cannot by my own reason or strength believe in Jesus Christ, my Lord, or come to Him. But the Holy Spirit has called me by the Gospel, enlightened me with His gifts, sanctified and kept me in the true faith. In the same way He calls, gathers, enlightens, and sanctifies the whole Christian Church on earth and keeps it with Jesus Christ in the one true faith. In this Christian Church He daily and richly forgives all my sins and the sins of all believers. On the Last Day He will raise up me and all the dead and will give eternal life to me to all believers in Christ. This is most certainly true.

The Large Catechism

Part II, Article III—The Apostles' Creed

I believe in the Holy Spirit, the holy Christian Church, the communion of saints, the forgiveness of sins, the resurrection of the body, and the life everlasting. Amen.

I cannot connect this article (as I have said) to anything better than Sanctification. Through this article the Holy Spirit, with His office, is declared and shown: He makes people holy [1 Corinthians 6:11]. Therefore, we must take our stand upon the term *Holy Spirit*, because it is so precise and complete that we cannot find another. For there are many kinds of spirits mentioned in the Holy Scriptures, such as the spirit of man [1 Corinthians 2:11], heavenly spirits [Hebrews 12:23], and evil spirits [Luke 7:21]. But God's Spirit alone is called the Holy Spirit, that is, He who has sanctified and still sanctifies us. For just as the Father is called "Creator" and the Son is called "Redeemer," so the Holy Spirit, from His work, must be called "Sanctifier," or "One who makes holy."

"But how is such sanctifying done?"

Answer, "The Son receives dominion, by which He wins us, through His birth, death, resurrection, and so on. In a similar way, the Holy Spirit causes our sanctification by the following: the communion of saints or the Christian Church, the forgiveness of sins, the resurrection of the body, and the life everlasting. That means He leads us first into His holy congregation and places us in the bosom of the Church. Through the Church He preaches to us and brings us to Christ."

Glossary

anti-authoritarianism. Narrowly defined, anti-authoritarianism is the rejection of any form of coercion or abuse of power, whether political, social, or economic. Broadly, anti-authoritarianism is the rejection of power held or used by another, whether an individual, group, or institution. See also **individualism.**

antinomianism. The teaching that the Law has no place in Christian proclamation or in the life of the believer. This view was championed by John Agricola at the time of the Reformation. It was rejected by both Luther and the Lutheran Confessions as it ultimately turned the Gospel into a new Law.

cafeterianism. An attempt to create one's own worldview by selecting, cafeteria-style, religious or moral concepts, ideas, and practices from a variety of sources. A person who attends a Christian church on Sunday while believing in reincarnation might be viewed as a "cafeterian," for example, since bodily resurrection and reincarnation are inherently incompatible.

efficacy of the Word. The power of God's Word to effect or accomplish its divine purpose.

enthusiasts. A term used by Luther to refer to the radical spiritualists who believed that God came to them apart from the external instruments of Word and Sacrament.

extra nos. Outside of us. Used to refer to the external character of the Gospel and Sacraments.

forensic justification. God renders a verdict that declares the unrighteous righteous for the sake of Jesus' atoning work on the cross.

humanism. A broad range of philosophies that emphasize human dignity and worth and recognize a common morality based on universal, rational human nature. Humanists who deny the possibility of any supernatural involvement in human affairs are sometimes called *secular* humanists.

individualism. A worldview emphasizing self-reliance and the achievement of personal goals or desires without the interference of society, the state, or other institutions. Individualism has been described by some philosophers, including Alexis de Tocqueville, as influencing a decline of society.

koinonia. The Greek term commonly translated in the Bible as communion, participation, sharing, or fellowship. *Koinonia* expresses a deep fellowship by faith between believers and their risen Lord, with His body and blood in the Lord's Supper, in His sufferings, death, and resurrection, and between believers and each other. This *koinonia*, beginning in Christ, expresses itself in concrete actions of charity and service for one's neighbor.

mysticism. While mysticism itself is a broad form of spirituality with distinct nuances, it is best characterized by the movement to transcend or move above the earthly through inward experience.

Office of the Keys. The authority that Christ has given His Church to unlock from their sins those who repent and to lock those who refuse to repent to their sins.

Pietism. A post-Reformation religious movement associated with Philip Spener (1635–1705) that was characterized by a shift from the objective reality of Christ's gifts to the subjective appropriation of the Gospel and the subsequent renewal of the believer's life personally and socially.

postmodernism. Refers to a cluster of themes that are somewhat interconnected in their opposition to the attempts to establish truthfulness that characterized the period of modernity. The focus of postmodernism is characterized by pluralism and the rejection of claims to absolute truth.

oratio, meditatio, tentatio. Prayer, meditation, and trial. Luther said that theologians (students of God's Word) are made by prayer, meditation, and the trial of life under the cross.

rationalism. The enlightenment movement that saw human reason as the ultimate criterion for reality.

revelation. God's act of making His will manifest in both Law and Gospel to human beings. The instrument of God's revelation is the prophetic and apostolic Scriptures.